Of rain

CW00501958

Susan Garman

Of rain and other things

For Anthony, Elizabeth and Michael

Thank you to
George Huitker
John Foulcher
Sally Mordike

Of rain and other things
ISBN 978 1 76109 403 3
Copyright © text Susan Garman 2022

First published 2022 by
GINNINDERRA PRESS
PO Box 3461 Port Adelaide 5015
www.ginninderrapress.com.au

Contents

Beach days

I never knew those beach days
would live until I was old

that other world at the coast
under a sun the city doesn't know

that caresses dreams undreamt
held tight by the raven night

we walked to the beach alone
wading in emptiness

melting feet from road to sand
the dunes, mysterious land

of sharp swaying grass
cutting our legs, crumbed and baked

telling childhood stories
with lips that had kissed

sucking our seaweed hair
and the ocean alive

swallowed us, white shiny shells
with cuttlebone hips

we would never again be free

Winter sun

Winter sits beside me
tangled in the garden
a child running in the wind

I hold a teacup with my grandmother's hands
the sun is warmer
than the deepest sleep

my lips open
as if they can keep this smudge of thought
from drifting away

Going home

After the storm the city gleams
sun trickles down towers of glass and steel

glimmering on tram tracks as people stitched
in unravelling lives scatter through streets

truant raindrops shot with light
diamonds that never land, split and bend

at the edge of all things, a circle of colour
chasing hearts that dream wider than eyes ever see

dusk falls, light blurs in shimmering lines
carrying you home, on the train

rocking out of town, in the jet of night

Waking

A white sheet covers the morning sky
it flaps on the line clapping against those days
when sails never docking bobbed on a watery horizon
when you wore a wedding gown in borrowed ivory
and a veil of lace that lay upon fruit trees
thwarting cockatoos which flash
high over green hills and blue bush in a sky whiter
than the picket fence and cricket gate you had to have
and at night, sleep sealed in hospital corners, you dream
and the sheet, splashed with morning, falls away

The orchestra

Twilight glimmers carelessly into the
day-wearied city casting its carnival colour
onto concrete streets once paved with gold
as lovers pour into the crimson hall lined
with dreams and mirrors to see and be seen
while the stolen silence listens
to the hum of messy lives, that cocktail of rush
that cannot be scrunched into a ball
and left in the cloakroom, they bunch
and tattle before scurrying to seats
still moving to the tune that streams
from buried megaphones, they come to sit
in the muted darkness, to hear

the oboe call across mountains and valleys
its sorrowful collect of galloping days
and endless nights, clear and known to rouse
bodies who wait, they draw and quiver
stretching souls, as winds crash upon jewelled rock
against a distant roll, so the orchestra of
whispering forests and roaming animals
eternal earth and soaring minds, wakes
and sounds its sounds, and for a time
emptiness is filled with beauty of no words
but thumping freedom until sands run clear
and in the white of endings and applause
champagne veneer settles snug and sure

Morning

the morning wakes
broken
and cries on fallen fruits
books half read
loved but left

what then of memory
of orange and blue
if the sun does not
lay down its swords
upon the grass

By the lake

From the skirts of trees
humble keepers of all you will never know
night's breath lounges on the still lake
as blessed youth lie late busy with heaven's hard labour
black swans crack the mirror kissed by clouds
while the urban bush beats, splashed
by red and yellow, survivors of the rainbow
passing souls teeter on the blue and the white
higher than dreams, cockatoos cry

Wattle

i.

Broken days creep by
not blind, not seeing
steady and true, leaving behind
land and lives burnt and stripped
bronzed leaves, laced in frost
cling in late winds as dormant days
in their passing, lament and bite
for they have seen the yellow bloom
in bush, invisible to concrete souls
golden galaxies hanging in wispy leaves
spinning in sounds soft and still
gentle warming days dripping in light
so the wattle grows

ii.

The day you left the wattle bloomed
yellow, older than the sun

sitting in days where cold flame burns
and deep dust dances

fading colour blots my tears
the world walks past the forgettable shrub

silence brings me back, it blooms
honey light in the darkness

iii.

I cannot not love
the wattle weed

scribbling gold
over dirt and stone

wild unwanted beauty
a little too much like me

Visiting the baby

Daphne blooms
I am on the bed
beyond tired
in some other place

I hear them arrive
people I do not know
to see the baby
new, anguished, mine

it is cold
she sleeps
shutting out people
crawling back into her soul

there is no time
it is night
it is light
I turn over

the path is wet
it has rained again
the curtains are thin
as slices of lemon in water

the doorbell rings
they wait
I hear them
admiring the daphne

Where flowers grow

At times I forget
the colour of spring leaves
the crash of rain
the frenzy of bees

the sun rose in another land
and followed me here

this road where flowers grow
where I walked
on petals fading into the memory of rainbows

if I stop
I would not breathe
what speck of dust flying in light
did I leave my soul in

it whispers
take off your shoes
the river will come to the road

Piano lessons

Homeless
with missing keys
voice of blunt hilarity
and an ebony coat
deep with the musk of days

the pianola
sat in the room
Dad built on weekends
a curiosity
a wonder
a door that swung open in a breeze
that swept dust and light and me

down the hill
to the piano teacher's house
past clipped brick dreams
under clear blue stars
stillness the only sound

and back up the hill
at night
released into darkness
dawdling home
under the wide engulfing sky

callow music quavered along
in the metallic glow of suburban beat
until I stood in the door
the stars far away
and turned my back
the door swinging on the hinge

Rewiring

the summer day is cold
like a lover who came to the door
without a word
rewired the house
then left some time ago

Of rain and other things

It was cloudy and warm that morning, already late
the air a whisper on my face, walking without a hat
for there was no sun, bliss really, after fifty years
of white heat burning the soles of pink feet
the rain fell fine at first, a balm pressing on my heart
the trees, always true in faithless weather, greener than frogs
and I imagined, as I walked, *this is what England is like*
I dreamed, I clambered, I wanted, but I did not know
for I have never stood in the woodland of bluebells and bramble
wandered the white coast and moor in light softer than self
the rain became heavy, washing me of everything decent
but in taking, left behind what cannot be washed away
a woman springs to mind, who lives in that cold wet land
and for a moment, like a star falling, I think
that could have been me, I could have left
now the jewels of that place, far away, that dribble through me
and of this place, where I have wandered, above and below me
the dirt and the trees, the rain and the light
lay scattered, solid and iridescent, illusive

Morning cup

the kettle boils
the day begins
a crystal stream pours
upon perfumed leaves
the earth and the sky within

scalded, they swirl
songs rise in the steam
the window is open
stillness moves
you listen to the green leaves chime
and the hum of the brew

Grey day

Rain fell in the night
waking the sun
sleepy and warm
in the tulle sky

jewels fall
from pale trees
the golden ground
tarnished in damp air
copper bells
only the child hears
trees of green
breathing their silent songs

who sees this day
this confusion of thorns
this dulled business of autumn
with no light to take the soul's hand
only the drizzle of life
it is enough
this grey, this beautiful day

On reading

The point of sale holds promise
Coloured light nudges sleeping books
holding the wonder and terror of life
A journey of dappled solitude begins
from peach skin to cherry wood to olive plastic
after the will has been read and pickings had

The point of sale is perfumed with virtue
It is not seen, covered in dust and inheritance
Not loaded with shiny thin copy
born of the shelter shed of us
the reassuring belonging of fraternity
It is almost given away the profound, the dense
the scribbled mind of a famous but unknown poet
a revered irrelevance in a world of bright tomorrows

The point of sale is touched by fear
The passing of money for an oblong fan of telling
raiser from dark to light
bridge from space to maze
Explosive enfolding words wait
while benevolent mocking voices huddle and scream
The voice that once was is read
It cannot be read in the crowded mind of day
when white light pastes newsprint onto the soul
and clarity is a loved one that abandons its young
Only in the dark early day
when yellow light hugs the black familiar silence
when the self does not exist, only the spirit

Then it can be read, those words
Words as familiar as the earth of your blood
carried and scattered upon the dust of others
where they have not been before
where they should not be
as told by mothers and fathers
who cared but never understood
Meaning rolls like a boiled lolly on a child's tongue
hard and impenetrable
worn to a wafer polished by time
or shattered into crystal shards
Then beauty, quivering in the forever world of cut and paste
rests within swirling peace

The point of sale is missed
the afternoon wastes away
day switches to night
The doors are locked

Have I ever seen

Have I ever seen
the blue of the sky
dusted in white
like today, over land
green and silver
rock older than light
silent trees
that call to me
as I walk the ground
achingly true
I have never known

Winter's end

Golden blooms herald
a gentle birth of days to come
as birdsong cracks the shell of sky

winter sways and weeps
heard only by skeleton trees
who have stood through dark days, they watch

but can do nothing for winter
forlorn as its white beauty wanes
for buds wake on brittle bones which ache for life

and into light, free from all things past
a meadow of trumpets forge through the floor
but they do not see the death of the old, for they are young

and too glad to sorrow, but spring
who knows they are one, embraces winter
and they dance for the last time, long and slow

the becoming and the ending
and all the while, time matted with fate circles
in an endless twist of swoon and fever, for they know

that the lovers will love and the piper is piping

Sunday walk

for Anthony

Battered hat on your head
the sun warm on your back
you walk to church

along summer's setting path
the lake shimmers
as you cross the bridge

and tune into words
sung from voices of other lands
streaming from the ether

your feet keep their rhythm
but your mind wanders
in this chapel without walls

passing a hall of green
the light softens
the earth is stealing you

the cockatoo chorale
sing in white robes
drowning the word of God

they rise
squabbling to themselves
and fly away

you reach the car
audio switches to stereo
the seamless flow of modernity

The clock

the clock
mid-century
hangs on
the wall
battering
thoughts
too fragile
to defy
the striking
blow of time
a metronome
is kinder

banished
the clock
still strikes
keeping time
you tell yourself
it will stop
as the sun
will rise
and the stars
will die
the clock
will stop

Growing up

It does not rain
where dreams begin
lying on wood
washed by sun
dancing dust and
smoke, sweet perfume
drifting into sound
quieter than silence

before the world
buckles under rain
great and grey
fine as your grip
scrambling for shelter
in concrete grottos
crushed by woollen
tattooed allegiants
horrifying familiar
strangers like you

Cherry

Cherry Anne Wolfe (1957–2020)

Before memory
you looked out into the world
through silver paper
a baby crossing the seas
a girl amongst adults
in a black and white world

I did not know you until later
in glorious colour
at Tagell Road
my grown up
wonderfully young aunt
whose name was simply Cherry

in the garden
an expanse of suburban green
the flowering edges
blood plums and climbing peas
the lawn and the willow tree
weeping upon the ground

living life
you were not always there
but I see you now
in the sun on a folding chair
in jeans and T-shirt
the lips of a Rolling Stone

you were, to me
a beautiful mystery
and the fine silver line
holds tight as
bohemian colour seeps
through days

and on the shelf
poetic cats and painted champagne glass
still sit
and sing with your voice

and at times I don't see coming
your smile
turns a corner
and your laugh
trickles by

A new friend

Along the way I saw you
not expecting anything new
but every step is a corner
and there you were, endearing
under the watchful leaves
of more classical trees
growing as the wind blows
shedding your bark
as you reached for the light
dancing in the park

Morning again

Morning again
you love me though I cry

thinking of the burnt wood
that cannot rest

how cold the water floats
I see but do not believe

great trees sway in wind
creaking at fine cracks

thundering trunks
holding the specks of ground

I walk on, as they fall
the air bites

pink clouds ripple the tender grey

Endings

the bin was out early
choking on yesterday

garnished with roses
cellophane dazzling in light

claret petals crash, irregularly
onto the melting road

November morning

November morning wakes me
with a gentleness closer
than any lover can ever reach

outside the young sky
swirls with colour painted
the palest tint of forever

and the night that was
lingers in the cool grass
I walk upon barefoot

crushing the diamond dew
that asks nothing of me
yet empties and fills my soul

and everywhere a beauty
runs about on young legs
forgotten hands reach out

to hold and a song I once knew
sings with a voice that brings
my beginning and end together

and nothing more is needed
for everything unbelieved
passes by on the soft breeze

Sweeping the leaves

She sweeps the leaves
on the pavement, in the gutter

sinking on the lawn
there's always a car passing

people walking, dogs shitting
do they see her efforts

that the path is clean of leaves
that the world is a better place

wrapped in aubergine velour
she looks down

her complimentary visor
blocks the sun that has risen again

even when the tree is empty
she sweeps the leaves

5.13 train

I saw a man at the station
his head in his hands
nothing but dust
a blur in the city
built from granules of earth
that were not meant for steel and glass

trains rock in and out
metal kissing metal
sparking fire
there is no other place
but this little scene
this man at the station
this man I do not know

Ash Wednesday

in the Quad

A wooden man stands silent
in the open
in the rain

curiosity hovers in blue stripes
balancing on concrete steps

a bowl cries
a few walk in the rain

most watch with flickering eyes
(can I see and not be seen?)

words are said
(can I hear and not be heard?)

ashes stick
a bell sounds
lunch ends

who chose this stage?
without walls
in the rain

Winter rose

When did my heart
become like the bones of roses
abandoned in autumn dusk
washed of warmth
forgotten strawberry of summer

left spindly and grey
to silver knives of air
slicing through moments that are left
to the sun crawling through cloud
towards the darkness of day

O shivering rose
shall I come back
as you who is cut down
and love the light
in colours that I dream of
after the chill of days?

In the marketplace

the piano
could be driftwood
sitting in the marketplace
left to float on waves
that have seen the horizon weep

the square
is crowded with space
drowning in sun

a child, floating on summer days
breathes light
her fingers touch the keys
notes rise and fall

people would not pay to hear
what fills the greater place
this colouring of land
this mosaic of sound
this wild dissonant harmony

The end of the day

White scribbled trees, common as dirt
stand tall in sacred bush as day looks back
remembering the morn and blushes gold
at its abandonment of the earth
and when the light is no more and the air
turns colder than the clearest mountain blue
drenched in sun that burns and chills
when the moon is the only hope that tomorrow
will exist as today and yesterday
the steel night deepens
and only the trees see the stars appear

Plum tree

Mother plum
your boughs
hang low in agony
touching the ground
birthing your royal fruit
those felted bulbs which carry
the yellow flesh of God

Mother plum
do you remember
the loveliness of spring
when bliss all white and pure
came upon you
when light shone
and rain fell upon your limbs

Mother plum
your fruit will fall
and feed the mouths of earth
your pain will pass
bliss will rust
and in mellow eve, will lay in wait
to love that loveliness once more

Five-thirty rain

Five-thirty rain sprinkles
through hessian sky
days abandoned by the sun

of blunt stone and dry pudding
in mouths that cannot swallow
waiting for light to knock

on the front door of houses
built by stories, told by puppets
and there in the rain

tears of heaven's heart
falling on the green commune of life
the prodigal sun returns

streaming through clouds
glistening, golden
standing free from walls

the garden gate
swings open on the post

Night washing

The washing machine
screams, the woman remembers

she hangs washing at night
with rainbow pegs
in the dark she is not seen

only by the moon
who holds her dreams
no longer under the bed
smelling of summer dust

the stars blink
she takes her time

Violin lessons

Lessons are on Fridays

the sky is blue
it is warm
at times I may faint
for it cannot be told
you must feel
you must find the note yourself
the dizziness of it all
the minutes swirl by

I leave shaking
at the edge of the forest I carry with me
the trees open
in survival, belief beats to a resounding drum
the earth spins
as if nothing has happened
magpies loiter
like school bullies waiting

I drive to the shops
folded in the car
I cry
I return with a tapping
a face at the window
a stranger, *am I all right*
my tears dry
does she cry
the neighbour looking out from the curtain
I'm fine, thank you
she leaves
she does not understand the weight of sound
scribbles on paper

Legacy

She left just paperback books
of no value
weighted with days
yellowing like skin
that no longer feels the prick of pins
but watch
gullies of dust chiselled with love
that never asked questions
a trail handwritten
in French, a heart
handed to you

Shiny midwinter

It is blue now
the afternoon leans on the sun
in love, shadows blush
the grass reels with the memory
of morning white, the rolling strudel clouds

as if the slant of light was not enough
shiny midwinter hums the sound of sand
sea birds swim through the coral sky
laughter tumbles down dunes
collecting in ebony pools

the olive sits in the silver air
it does not remember yesterday or see tomorrow
moments convalesce
in earth as warm as apricots
the day never ages, dying before it is old

White birds

White birds
circle the sky
in trees you know well

they might be angels
wings sweeping
the falling light

people walk past
lives must be lived
there is nothing to see

but white birds
flying away

Rain in white clouds

Days are long gone and
nights no longer a memory
and still I walk upon land
I do not know in a stranger's soul
drowning in resurrection
whispering its story to the
rising sea of white morning
blinding the requiem of stars
which pours over me as I fall
and cry at clustered chords
spun in the mines of heaven
for I am frailer than a lily
dancing in storms
that quake the earth
with only crumbs to hold it
wandering through cities of sand
lost in light ringing
with the wizardry of cicada song
and my cage is all I have
sweet wilderness
bird and insect, tree and rock
sizzling bush
for it only takes a moment for
rain to fall from white clouds
and butterflies to cross your path

Snow on the daffodils

Today a cockatoo flew
across a scalloped sky
through the pink silence
of the correa bell

waking the raindrop
white, crystal moon
from its cherry slumber
as still as my heart

in the hands of rock
remembering when snow
fell on the daffodils
and sadness cried its yellow tears

The dawn is white

The dawn is white
dusted in sugar
and dipped in milk

berries of light
rain on the earth
whispers of leaves float in

the thoughts of a soul
walking in woods, on cobbled streets
years ago, today

the eucalypt, touches the sky
weeping, where grass grows green
there is silence

except for the birds
that sing after the heart lays down
on the soft ground

Elastic pearls

Sometimes I glimpse
the darkness of silk
the sound of dawn
painting the sky

I long for blossom
but it is the cindered eucalypt
I hear, its cello soul
long and deep

moments that were mine
and yours, those elastic pearls
guzzled, at times spilt
ripple in the pages of my bones

I sit with death
my companion now
smelling of wood and honey
looking through venetian blinds

the sun is low and tangerine
it dances
perhaps eternity is just another moment
wondrous and frayed

CPSIA information can be obtained
at www.ICGtesting.com
Printed in the USA
LVHW012055101022
730380LV00013B/531